Global Issues

Natural Heritage

Cheryl Jakab

MACMILLAN
LIBRARY

First published in 2010 by
MACMILLAN EDUCATION AUSTRALIA PTY LTD
15–19 Claremont Street, South Yarra 3141

Visit our website at www.macmillan.com.au or go directly to www.macmillanlibrary.com.au

Associated companies and representatives throughout the world.

National Library of Australia Cataloguing-in-Publication entry

Jakab, Cheryl.
   Natural heritage / Cheryl Jakab.
   ISBN: 9781420267426 (hbk.)
   Series: Global issues; set 3
   Includes index.
   Target Audience: For primary school age.
   Subjects: Natural areas—Juvenile literature. Natural resources—Juvenile literature. Environmental
   protection—Juvenile literature. Conservation of natural resources—Juvenile literature.
333.72

Edited by Margaret Maher
Text and cover design by Cristina Neri, Canary Graphic Design
Page layout by Domenic Lauricella
Photo research by Sarah Johnson
Illustrations by Domenic Lauricella
Maps courtesy of Geo Atlas

Printed in China

Acknowledgements
The author and the publisher are grateful to the following for permission to reproduce copyright
material:

Front cover photograph: Caves in Gunung Mulu National Park, © Tony Walthan/Jupiter Images

© Bob Krist/CORBIS, 28; © Galen Rowell/CORBIS, 16; © Paul A. Souders/CORBIS, 18; Image
© J.Cunningham (1965), 21 (right); Image © R. Duffy (1999), 7 (top), 21 (left); Elphinstone Landcare
group in Elphinstone, central Victoria. Photo: Elizabeth Mellick, 19; Charles Bowman/Getty Images, 5;
National Geographic/Getty Images, 6 (top), 25; © Kristian Larsen/iStockphoto, 6 (bottom left), 9;
© Tarzan9280/iStockphoto, 10; © Corbis/Jupiter Images, 6 (bottom right), 8, 13; © Thorsten Milse /
Jupiter Images, 7 (bottom), 17; © Hemera Technologies /Jupiter Images, 24; © Tony Waltham /Jupiter
Images, 23; Dave Fleetham/Pacific Stock/Photolibrary, 15; Adam Jones/Photo Researchers/Photolibrary,
20, 26; © Wolfgang Amri/Shutterstock, 12; © Sebastien Burel/Shutterstock, 29; © capturefoto/
Shutterstock, 11; © GagarinART/Shutterstock, 27; © David V/Shutterstock, 22.

While every care has been taken to trace and acknowledge copyright, the publisher tenders their
apologies for any accidental infringement where copyright has proved untraceable. Where the attem pt
has been unsuccessful, the publisher welcomes information that would redress the situation.

Please note
At the time of printing, the Internet addresses appearing in this book were correct. Owing to the dynamic
nature of the Internet, however, we cannot guarantee that all these addresses will remain correct.

Contents

Glossary words
When a word is printed in **bold**, you can look up its meaning in the Glossary on page 31.

Facing global issues

Hi there! This is Earth speaking. Will you spare a moment to listen to me? I have some very important things to discuss.

We must face up to some urgent environmental problems! All living things depend on my environment, but the way you humans are living at the moment, I will not be able to keep looking after you.

The issues I am worried about are:

- large ecological footprints
- damage to natural heritage sites
- widespread pollution in the environment
- the release of **greenhouse gases** into the **atmosphere**
- poor management of wastes
- environmental damage caused by food production.

My challenge to you is to find a **sustainable** way of living. Read on to find out what people around the world are doing to try to help.

Fast fact

Concerned people in local, national and international groups are trying to understand how our way of life causes environmental problems. This important work helps us learn how to live more sustainably now and in the future.

What's the issue?
Natural heritage in danger

Today, some of the most spectacular natural heritage sites on Earth are in danger of damage by people. These sites urgently need protection.

What are natural heritage sites?

Natural heritage sites are places with significant natural value. They may contain important examples of:

- natural **biological features** or **geological features**
- threatened **habitats**, plants or animal **species**
- natural areas of scientific, conservational or **aesthetic value**.

Protecting natural heritage

Natural heritage sites urgently need protection. Human populations across the world are spreading out into the remaining natural areas. Protecting these areas can prevent damage and loss of significant natural sites.

Heritage is what we get from the past and pass on to future generations. People of the future have a right to enjoy natural heritage sites, as we do today.

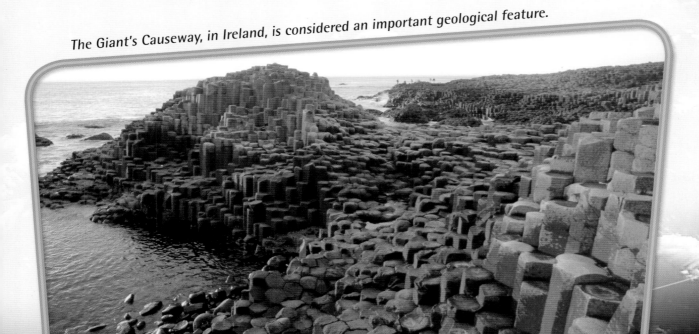

The Giant's Causeway, in Ireland, is considered an important geological feature.

Natural heritage issues

The most urgent natural heritage issues around the globe include:

- tourism and **introduced pest species** endangering unique island species (see issue 1)
- **over-fishing** and **global warming** damaging coral reefs (see issue 2)
- population pressures reducing land for wildlife (see issue 3)
- rare and unusual habitats damaged by visitors (see issue 4)
- geological sites damaged by tourism (see issue 5).

N O R T H

A M E R I C A

United States

N O R T H

A T L A N T I

O C E A N

Caribbean Sea

Galapagos Islands

ISSUE 5
United States
Tourism is damaging the Grand Canyon. See pages 24–27.

ISSUE 1
Galapagos Islands
Rare species are being threatened by introduced pest species and tourism. See pages 8–11.

ISSUE 2
Caribbean Sea
Over-fishing, pollution and global warming are damaging coral reefs. See pages 12–15.

around the globe

Fast fact
The first 12 World Heritage sites were listed in 1978. Some sites, such as the Galapagos Islands, were listed for their natural heritage. Others, such as the churches of Lalibela in Ethiopia, were listed for their cultural heritage. This is heritage created by the actions or cultures of people.

England

E U R O P E

N O R T H

P A C I F I C

Tropic of Cancer

O C E A N

ISSUE 4

England
Formations in **cave systems** are being damaged by visitors. See pages 20–23.

A F R I C A

Democratic Republic of the Congo

Equator

I N D I A N

O C E A N   AUSTRALIA

ISSUE 3

Democratic Republic of the Congo
Wildlife and habitat in Virunga National Park are threatened by increasing human populations. See pages 16–19.

Island species in danger

Many islands have a great range of unique plants and animals. These are an important part of the world's natural heritage. However, many species of plants and animals found only on World Heritage listed islands are **endangered**.

Biodiversity on islands

Islands and the waters around them are rich in **biodiversity**. Although these areas make up only one-sixth of Earth's surface, they contain more than half the world's sea life.

Threats to island life

Introduced pest species and tourism are the major threats to island **ecosystems**. They can damage habitats and disturb native animals. **Unsustainable development** and habitat destruction, such as clearing land for farms, also threaten island ecosystems.

Fast fact
The most famous **extinction** of all was of an island species called the dodo. The dodo became extinct only about 100 years after it was first seen by Europeans on the island of Mauritius.

The komodo dragon is an endangered species found only in the islands of Indonesia.

Many species on the Galapagos Islands, such as the small tree finch, live nowhere else on Earth.

CASE STUDY
The Galapagos Islands

The Galapagos Islands are very isolated islands in the Pacific Ocean, 1000 kilometres off the coast of South America. These islands were the first natural World Heritage site listed, in 1978.

The Galapagos Islands are world famous for their biodiversity. There are rare species of birds and reptiles on each island.

Threats to the islands

Tourism is the major threat to the Galapagos Islands today. The tourism industry has encouraged development and population growth, which means more land is cleared for housing and farming. Introduced pest species, such as goats, are also destroying the islands' habitats and biodiversity.

Fast fact
The number of people visiting the Galapagos Islands each year increased from 40 000 in 1996 to 120 000 in 2007. The local population is increasing by 4 per cent every year.

Towards a sustainable future: Valuing island ecosystems

Today there is greater awareness that island ecosystems are valuable. They contain a large part of the world's biological natural heritage.

List of World Heritage in Danger

The Galapagos Islands have been added to the List of World Heritage in Danger. This means that, unless there is an improvement in conservation, the site will lose its World Heritage listing. It alerts the world to the need for urgent action and gives the islands extra protection.

Global Island Partnership

In 2005, the Global Island Partnership was called for by the Seychelles and Palau. These island nations were urgently in need of assistance to protect their natural heritage. The Global Island Partnership led to the creation of a United Nations program to manage island biodiversity sustainably.

Fast fact

Adding the Galapagos Islands to the List of World Heritage in Danger focused attention on damage from tourism. It also highlighted the need to change the way tourism is managed.

The Seychelles giant tortoise, part of the Seychelles' natural heritage, was thought to be extinct until 1997.

Habitat conservation on Madagascar helps protect many lemurs, including the ring-tailed lemur.

CASE STUDY

Conserving Madagascar's rainforests

Madagascar is an island off the coast of south-eastern Africa. It has a rich variety of wildlife and up to 10 000 species of plants. The rainforests of Madagascar are now one of the highest conservation priorities in the world.

Extinctions on Madagascar

There have been many extinctions on Madagascar since the arrival of humans less than 2000 years ago. They include a lemur the size of a gorilla, a pygmy hippo, the largest flightless bird in the world and giant tortoises.

Conservation efforts

In recent years Madagascar has become well known for conservation efforts. These efforts focus on the habitat of lemurs. Black-and-white ruffed lemurs have been bred in captivity to increase their numbers. The first of these lemurs were released into the wild in 1997.

Coral reefs under threat

Coral reefs are marine habitats formed by animals called coral polyps. Many of these reefs are now under threat due to over-fishing, pollution and global warming.

Coral habitats

The best-known reef-building coral polyps live in habitats of shallow, warm tropical waters. Many animals and plants live on or around coral reefs, including species people take as food.

Damage to coral reefs

Over-fishing, pollution and even mining are damaging coral reefs across the globe. Most coral polyps live in only a narrow range of temperatures. This puts reefs at risk of damage from global warming.

The damage to coral reefs threatens biodiversity and ecosystems around the reefs. The death of a reef destroys the habitat of plants and animals that live there. It also threatens people who depend on the reef for food.

Fast fact

The UNEP World Conservation Monitoring Centre began mapping coral reefs in 1994. It has produced global maps of coral reefs in the World Atlas of Coral Reefs, available online.

Coral reefs provide habitat for thousands of species of animals and plants.

If parrotfish numbers decline, the health of coral reefs will suffer.

CASE STUDY
Declining coral reefs

There has been a dramatic decline in the health of coral reefs in the Caribbean Sea over the last 25 years. Many corals have died.

Coral damage

In the 1980s, reefs in the Caribbean were devastated by the near-extinction of a sea urchin. This urchin ate seaweed on the reefs, creating space for coral polyps to grow.

Parrotfish are now the only seaweed grazers on many Caribbean reefs. If parrotfish numbers drop due to over-fishing, the seaweed will take over and coral polyps will die.

Coral bleaching

Coral bleaching occurs when coral polyps are stressed. The polyps expel the colourful algae that live inside them and soon die. Between 1998 and 2004, there were five major bleaching events in the Caribbean. In 2005, a massive bleaching was followed by disease and coral death.

Fast fact
Protecting living things in the open ocean is difficult. This is because whaling and fishing cannot easily be controlled in areas far from land.

13

Towards a sustainable future: Caring for marine heritage

Marine heritage areas close to land, including coral reefs, are now getting more attention. However other marine areas also need protection.

Adding to heritage lists

About 200 World Heritage sites are listed for their natural values. Of these, only 31 are protected for their marine biodiversity. In 2002, UNESCO began exploring ways to add more tropical coastal, marine and small island ecosystems to the World Heritage List. Many areas were identified, but as of 2009 only four had been listed.

Other marine areas

Marine heritage areas away from coasts need protection too. They are threatened by pollution, deep-sea mining and fishing. All the World Heritage listed marine areas today are close to land.

Fast fact
The Exuma Cays Land and Sea Park in the Bahamas limits fishing, and commercial fishing is banned. The number of young coral polyps in this park is increasing.

This map shows the current marine World Heritage sites.

Natural System of Wrangel Island Reserve

High Coast

Glacier Bay

St Kilda

EUROPE

ASIA

Cape Girolata, Cape Porto, Scandola Nature Reserve and the Piana Calanches in Corsica

Shiretoko

NORTH AMERICA

Whale Sanctuary of El Vizcaino

Sian Ka'an   Belize Barrier Reef

Desembarco del Granma National Park

Banc d'Arguin National Park

AFRICA

Islands and Protected Areas of the Gulf of California

Pitons Management Area

Tubbataha Reef Marine Park

Area de Conservación Guanacaste

Cocos Island National Park

SOUTH AMERICA

Brazilian Atlantic Islands

Ujung Kulon

East Rennel

Galapagos Islands

Aldabra Atoll

Komodo National Park

Great Barrier Reef

Coiba National Park and its Special Zone of Marine Protection

Shark Bay

AUSTRALIA

Greater St Lucia Wetland Park

Peninsula Valdes

Gough and Inaccessible Islands

Heard and McDonald Islands   Macquarie Island   New Zealand Sub-Antarctic Islands

ANTARCTICA

The Great Barrier Reef is the largest World Heritage site.

CASE STUDY

Managing the Great Barrier Reef

The Great Barrier Reef in Australia is the largest coral reef system in the world. It is more than 2000 kilometres long. The site is managed by the Great Barrier Reef Marine Park Authority (GBRMPA).

Protecting the Great Barrier Reef

The GBRMPA uses a system of zoning to protect the Great Barrier Reef. Different areas can be used for different purposes, such as general use, boating, fishing and research. Some parts of the reef have full protection and may not be used for any of these purposes.

Reporting on the reef

The GBRMPA must report regularly to the World Heritage Committee on the state of the reef. These reports are used to help plan the management of the Great Barrier Reef.

Fast fact
In 1996 the Belize Barrier Reef Reserve System was granted World Heritage listing. It is the largest barrier reef in the Northern Hemisphere.

Wildlife habitat under pressure

Some wildlife, such as large herd animals and **migratory birds**, need large areas of habitat. However, this habitat in deserts, forests and **rangelands** is under pressure from people.

Land habitat under threat in Africa

In the past, large areas of land in Africa provided habitat for huge numbers of animals. Today, these areas are being taken over by people.

Threats from people

The main threat comes from the rapidly increasing human population. Today there are so many people that competition for land is great. Animal habitat is often used for farming and building homes, particularly in areas where people are poor. Large land animals are also being hunted. Other threats from people include pollution, **poaching** and unplanned construction.

Fast fact

In 2007, UNESCO removed the Arabian Oryx Sanctuary in Oman from the World Heritage List. This was because Oman had not cared for the area. It was the first time a site had ever been deleted from the list.

African zebras and wildebeests need large areas of habitat to graze, but these areas are being reduced by increasing human populations.

Virunga National Park is one of only a few places where mountain gorillas can still be found.

CASE STUDY

Virunga National Park

Virunga National Park is in the Democratic Republic of the Congo. It contains the greatest diversity of habitats of any park in Africa. However, it is now threatened by increased numbers of people.

World heritage in danger

Virunga National Park was placed on the List of World Heritage in Danger in 1994, after a civil war in Rwanda. Millions of refugees came to the Democratic Republic of the Congo for safety.

The increase in refugees resulted in increased poaching and forest clearing in the park. People who were forced to leave their homes began to use the park habitat for their own needs. Forests were cut down for fuel, and thousands of hippopotamus were killed. The gorillas that live in the park were threatened by loss of habitat and poaching.

Towards a sustainable future: Protecting large areas

Setting aside large areas as natural heritage sites is difficult when people are in need. However, it is a vital first step to saving many unique ecosystems across the world.

Importance of large areas

Large areas are important as habitats for large mammals and migratory birds on each continent. These animals depend on large expanses of land to survive. Because of this, they need protection from the pressure of increasing human populations.

Protection from rapid population growth

Many areas in Asia and Africa are threatened by rapid population growth. Large areas on each continent need to be protected for their natural heritage value. They can then be set aside before further development occurs.

Fast fact

Two large-area sites were removed from the List of World Heritage in Danger in 2007. They were the Río Plátano Biosphere Reserve in Honduras and the Florida Everglades National Park. Each site has been improved, so they are no longer in danger.

Large mammals, such as moose, need large areas of habitat to provide them with enough food.

Recording protected vegetation helps people decide where conservation efforts, such as tree planting, are needed.

CASE STUDY

Connecting Country

Connecting Country is a large-area conservation project in Victoria, in south-eastern Australia.

Biodiversity crisis

Victoria is the most cleared state in Australia. Few large areas of forests and grasslands remain. About a third of its native animals are either threatened or extinct. The native plants are in even worse condition. **Habitat fragmentation**, the spread of weeds and introduced pest species have created an environmental crisis.

Recording protected vegetation

The Connecting Country project is recording areas of protected vegetation across central Victoria. This will create a computer database to show all private and public conservation areas.

Natural habitats in central Victoria are severely fragmented. Mapping conservation areas shows where there are gaps. This allows people to see where more conservation efforts are needed.

Threats to hidden areas

Many natural heritage areas are hidden underground, in jungles and under oceans. These include cave systems, rare animal habitats and deep-sea animal communities around **hydrothermal vents**.

Damage to hidden heritage

Many areas of hidden heritage are being damaged, sometimes before people even know what is there. Ocean floors, for example, are being mined and fished by damaging processes. Often, more damage is done by people when they find these hidden treasures. Sometimes the damage is deliberate. At other times it is simply careless, or due to large numbers of admiring visitors.

Cave systems

Many cave systems have been added to the World Heritage List for their cultural and natural values. These values include geological features, natural beauty, biodiversity and habitat for threatened species.

Ancient cave systems, such as Mammoth Cave in the US, are popular tourist sites.

Some World Heritage listed caves		
Name	**Country**	**Main heritage feature**
Mammoth Cave	US	Significant natural formations
Cave of Altamira	Spain	14 000-year-old cave paintings
Mogao Caves	China	Statues and wall paintings spannir 1000 years of Buddhist art
Elephanta Caves	India	Rock art linked to the cult of Shiv:
Naracoorte Caves	Australia	Complete fossil record

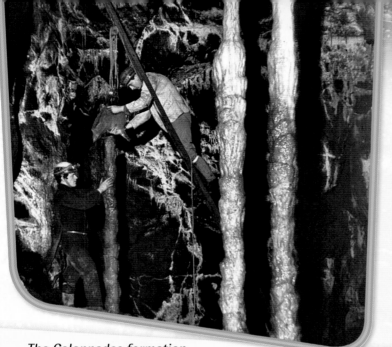

The Colonnades formation at Ease Gill had to be repaired after it was broken by a visitor.

The repaired column can now be seen by visitors.

CASE STUDY

Damage to the Ease Gill cave system

The Ease Gill cave system in England has been named a Site of Special Scientific Interest because of its plants, animals and geological features. However, carelessness and deliberate damage have had huge impacts on this important cave system.

Damage by visitors

Some of the most spectacular formations in the cave system have been damaged by vandalism and careless or thoughtless visitors. This includes the Angel's Wing and Colonnades formations.

Preserving the Ease Gill cave system

Preserving the natural heritage of the Ease Gill cave system is important. The ancient rivers, stalagmites and gravels in the cave system can give information about past climates. Tourism is welcomed to let the public connect with nature. However, it needs to be carefully controlled to avoid further damage.

Fast fact
In 2006, a rock containing a 200-million-year-old fossilised dinosaur footprint was advertised on eBay. It had been stolen from Bendrick Rock, a protected site in Wales.

Towards a sustainable future: Sustainable tourism

Tourism can bring important funds to support World Heritage sites, but it must be carefully managed to ensure it is sustainable.

Managing tourism

Adding a site to the World Heritage List increases public awareness of the site and its values. However, the increase in tourists visiting the site needs to be carefully managed so the site is protected. In cave systems, this can be done by providing paths and erecting barriers. This limits the areas where tourists can walk. It can guide tourists through areas and reduce damage to the site.

Tourism can help local communities living in or near World Heritage sites, particularly in **developing countries**. It can provide jobs and bring money into the area. However, poorly managed tourism can do irreversible damage to heritage sites. Isolated and hidden sites are particularly open to damage, because guarding them can be costly.

Fast fact
The Sichuan Giant Panda Sanctuaries in China were added to the World Heritage List in 2007. Visitors can now see pandas and even help with their care.

Fragile cave systems can be protected from damage by the installation of pathways and fencing.

The number of visitors to the caves in Gunung Mulu National Park is limited to protect the site.

CASE STUDY
Gunung Mulu National Park

Gunung Mulu National Park is on the island of Borneo. It is famous for its cave systems. Transport is improving in the area, so more people are able to visit the park. This has made the site vulnerable to damage.

Outstanding heritage features

Gunung Mulu National Park was given World Heritage listing in 2000. Its outstanding feature is the number of caves it contains. The cave called the Sarawak Chamber is the largest known cave chamber in the world.

Protecting the site

World Heritage listing helps protect the site from the impacts of visitors. It assists in getting donations to pay for conservation. It also limits the legal use of sites. This means the number of visitors is limited to prevent damage.

Fast fact
The Jeju volcanic island and lava tubes in Korea were named a World Heritage site in 2007. They are described as the finest lava tube system of caves in the world.

Protecting geological sites

Geological sites include places where landscapes created by erosion, volcanic activity and **glaciers** can be seen. They also include sites containing fossils. Today, many of the most spectacular geological sites on Earth need protection from the impacts of tourism. Tour operators organise tours so visitors can experience these wonders of nature. However, some operators run tours that damage the very environment tourists are interested in visiting.

Damage to geological sites

Rocks are hard and appear difficult to damage. However, poorly run tourism can cause damage and reduce the heritage value of sites. This damage can be permanent, such as the impact of thousands of people walking on tracks. It can also be something that makes a visit to the site less enjoyable for others. For example, noisy vehicles can disturb the environment.

Fast fact
For at least 500 000 years the Naracoorte Caves in South Australia trapped animals that fell into them and formed fossils over time. In 1994 they were given World Heritage listing for their complete fossil record.

Dinosaur Provincial Park, in Canada, is an important geological site that contains fossils 75 million years old.

Many people like to take flights over the Grand Canyon, but noise from planes disturbs other visitors.

CASE STUDY
Noise in the Grand Canyon

Noise from tourism is damaging the Grand Canyon in the US, one of the most well-known geological World Heritage sites.

The Grand Canyon

The Grand Canyon has been carved out by the Colorado River over thousands of years. It is nearly 1500 metres deep. The natural quiet in the canyon is said to be astounding. Many people believe this is an important part of visiting the canyon.

Noise in the Grand Canyon

Today, the silence is gone. Instead, the noise of tourist flights fills the canyon. In 1987, the government passed a law to restore natural quiet to the park. On Earth Day in 1996, President Clinton ordered a limit on numbers of sightseeing aircraft. However, flights over and through the canyon continue to increase, as does the noise.

Fast fact
The sides of the Grand Canyon contain layers of coloured rock. These layers expose the **geological history** of site for the past 2 billion years.

Towards a sustainable future: Ongoing protection

Protecting world heritage, including geological sites, is an ongoing process. It is supported by the United Nations and many groups across the world.

Protecting world heritage

The Convention Concerning the Protection of World Cultural and Natural Heritage protects World Heritage sites, such as the Grand Canyon. Under this convention, countries must inform UNESCO of any threats to their World Heritage sites. Threats include noise and visual pollution, as well as more direct physical damage or destruction of sites.

Balanced heritage listing

In its first 20 years the World Heritage List lacked balance. Of the 410 sites, only 90 were natural. Most were located in **developed countries**. In 1994, the World Heritage Committee began trying to fix this problem. Natural and geological sites across all parts of the world are now being listed.

Rangers at heritage sites, such as Mammoth Cave, can check to make sure the site is not being damaged.

Fast fact
The World Heritage fossil sites of Sterkfontein, Swartkrans and Kromdraai in South Africa are part of the 'Cradle of Humankind'. Remains of some of the earliest human ancestors are preserved at these sites.

Cruise boat tours are now limited in Geirangerfjord and Nærøyfjord.

CASE STUDY

World Heritage listed fjord formations

Fjords are deep valleys, cut by glaciers, that have filled with seawater. Two of Norway's most scenic fjords, Geirangerfjord and Nærøyfjord, were added to the World Heritage List in 2005.

Geirangerfjord and Nærøyfjord

Geirangerfjord and Nærøyfjord are two of the world's longest and deepest fjords. They are 120 kilometres apart and are separated by the Jostedal glacier. They were the first heritage sites in Norway chosen for their natural and geological value.

A popular place to visit

The Geirangerfjord and Nærøyfjord areas are very popular with tourists. They are considered to be among the most scenic fjord areas on the planet. Heritage listing focuses attention on the need to control tourism, particularly the noise from cruise ships travelling up the fjords. Listing as a World Heritage site means tourism is more strictly controlled.

Fast fact

Due to concern about global warming, some environmental campaigners want Mount Everest placed on the List of World Heritage in Danger.

What can you do?
Learn about sustainable tourism

Much of the damage done by tourists is due to lack of knowledge. When you visit a site, make sure you learn about sustainable tourism. This means making sure your travel will support the local community and will not harm the site.

Build rules for sustainable tourism

Use the list below to help you build your own rules for sustainable tourism. Look at tourist brochures advertising a heritage site you would like to visit. Evaluate the tours using your list, to see if they support sustainable tourism.

Sustainable tourism rules

- Inform yourself of the environmental impacts of your visits.
- Learn about the heritage value of the sites you are visiting.
- Travel outside the peak seasons to avoid overcrowding.
- Use local guides and accommodation that return profits to the community.
- Show respect for local cultural heritage and the environment.
- Buy local products and pay a fair price to producers.
- Visit local sites that conserve nature and culture.

Many heritage areas have information centres where you can learn about the site you are visiting.

You can study the natural heritage of your local area or a World Heritage site near your home.

Create a tourist brochure

Each area has distinct cultural and natural heritage. Create a tourist brochure for a World Heritage site in your local area, state or country. Advertise the special features that make it (or could make it) of world heritage value. These may be geological, biological or cultural heritage features. The example below focuses on geological and landscape heritage.

Geological and landscape heritage

Make a list of the major geological or landscape features in your chosen area. Think about the following information for your brochure:

- What mountains, volcanoes, gorges, rock formations or other features are of interest?
- How big are these compared to others in World Heritage areas?
- What types of rocks are there?
- How can you find out how old these rocks are and how they formed?

Fast fact
The United Nations heritage convention describes heritage as both cultural and natural. This is to remind people that it is important to maintain a balance between humans and nature.

Towards a sustainable future

Well, I hope you now see that if you take up my challenge your world will be a better place. There are many ways to work towards a sustainable future. Imagine it... a world with:

- a sustainable ecological footprint
- places of natural heritage value protected for the future
- no more environmental pollution
- less greenhouse gas in the air, reducing global warming
- zero waste and efficient use of resources
- a secure food supply for all.

This is what you can achieve if you work together with my natural systems.

We must work together to live sustainably. That will mean a better environment and a better life for all living things on Earth, now and in the future.

Websites

For further information on natural heritage, visit the following websites.

- Our Place: The World Heritage Collection
  www.ourplaceworldheritage.com/index.cfm?&action=ourplace
- United Nations Environment Programme World Conservation Monitoring Centre www.unep-wcmc.org/index.html
- UNESCO photo bank http://photobank.unesco.org/exec/index.htm
- Earth Science World Image Bank www.earthscienceworld.org/images/

Glossary

aesthetic value
the value placed on a site for its beauty

atmosphere
the layers of gases surrounding the Earth

biodiversity
the range of living things in an area

biological features
the living things that are significant or typical in an area

cave systems
complexes of large, connected caves or holes in the ground

developed countries
countries with industrial development, a strong economy and a high standard of living

developing countries
countries with less developed industry, a poor economy and a lower standard of living

ecosystems
all the living and non-living things in an area, and their connections with each other

endangered
at a high likelihood of becoming extinct

extinction
loss of a species when all its members die out

geological features
landscape features made up of rocks and soil

geological history
the history of the rocks and other geological features of an area

glaciers
rivers of moving ice

global warming
an increase in the average temperature on Earth

greenhouse gases
gases that help trap heat in Earth's atmosphere

habitat fragmentation
breaking up large areas of habitat into smaller areas, for example by clearing parts of a forest

habitats
the areas used by living things to provide for their needs

hydrothermal vents
cracks in the Earth's surface underneath the sea, where the water is warmed by the heat inside the Earth

introduced pest species
a non-native species that damages the environment

migratory birds
birds that live in different regions at different seasons

over-fishing
taking too many fish from one area or species, leading to a decrease in numbers

poaching
taking or killing wildlife illegally

rangelands
broad areas of land used by grazing animals; can be made up of grasslands, forests and scrublands

species
living things of the same type that can breed and reproduce

sustainable
does not use more resources than the Earth can regenerate

threatened species
a species that is likely to become endangered

unsustainable development
developing industry, tourism and standards of living in a way that uses more resources than the Earth can regenerate

Index